To

_____

From

_____

Date

_____

Upcoming Books by
Shakisha Shamain Edness

Women Overcoming Weight-loss Journal
Women Overcoming Weight-loss Workbook
Break Through Volume I & II
Break Through I & II Workbook
Uncovering Me through Poetry
A Christmas to Remember
From the Eyes of a Child
A Man Can Only Do What a Woman Allows

Women Overcoming WEIGHT LOSS

Strengthening the Mind, Body & Soul

P.E.M.S.

see pg 13

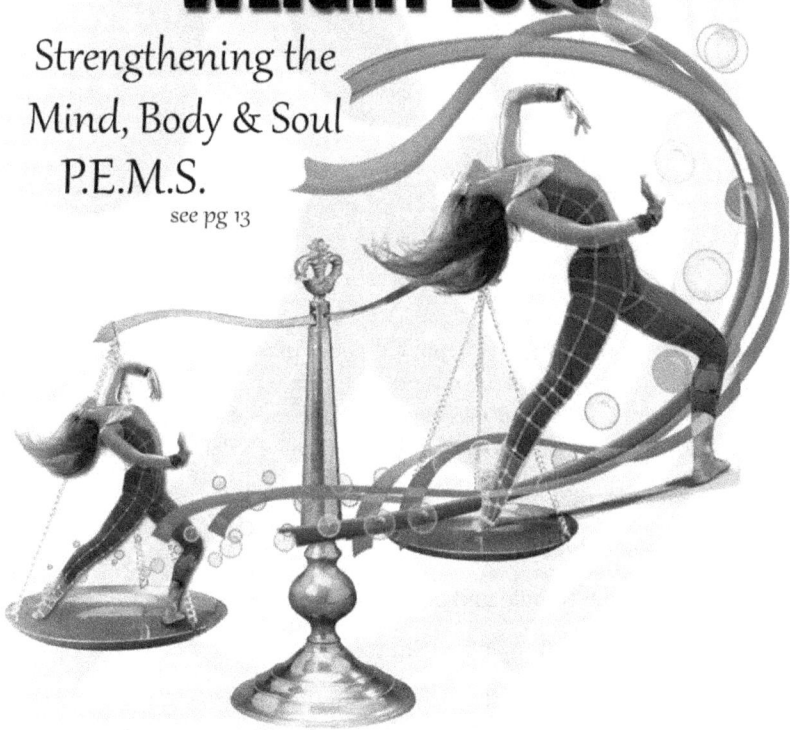

Shakisha Edness

WOMEN OVERCOMING WEIGHT-LOSS

Cover design: Jacobie Brown

Editor: Shanice Edness

Cover illustration: Google and Shutterstock

Interior illustration: Google and Shutterstock

Interior design: T.R.A.C Publishing

Bible Scriptures: New Living Translation

Definitions: Webster's Dictionary and Google

ISBN: 10: 0692025383

ISBN-13: 978-0692-02538-3

Library of Congress catalog card number:

Printed in the United States of America

DEDICATION

I **dedicate this** book to my mother and grandmother, Tracie and Rhoda Edness, that I have seen overcome many obstacles in their lives.

To my daughters, Shukriyyah and Shanice Edness, I love you and hope you both will allow this book to help you lose weight emotionally, mentally, and physically!

May this book bless my baby sister, Shahidah Edness, in a supernatural way!

To my brother, Shakim Edness, I love as my own son, "Though this book is for women, I'm sure it can be such a blessing to men as well!"

To my uncle T.J, "Tamajian Edness, I love you so much!"

Richard Gibbs Jr., my son, "Thanks for everything! You are the air that I breathe."

To a host of family and friends, "I love you!"

ACKNOWLEDGMENTS

I am acknowledging my Lord and Savior Jesus Christ. He is the only Man that has ever carried weight and the pressures of the world, which He never deserved. It was not for Him; but for us. He never complained, because of the love He has for us. So He endured it until the end.

When He died on the cross, was it the end? No. Remember He rose on the third day! Will you rise above the weights? I did and not by my might or power, but Jesus!

Thank you Jesus; for removing the weights holding me down. Thanks for strengthening me to be able to lift the weights; that you ordered to take me to the next level. I could not lose physical, mental, or emotional weight without you. I love you and thank you for first loving me! Amen.

Lord, thank you for everything you have done, are doing, and will do in my life! Thank you for forgiving me, when I did not know how to forgive myself. Thanks for your protection, guidance, and wisdom.

He tried to save me much sooner, but God will not force you to choose Him; but you will wish you had. God is jealous and He does not want you to put people or things before Him, so Keep Him First!

CONTENTS

INTRODUCTION

Let me give you a brief description of **Women Overcoming**. Let me tell you how **WEIGHT LOSS** was birthed out of **Women Overcoming**. Are you familiar with the statement, "I was lost but now I am found?" Well, I was lost and God allowed me to find Him. In finding Him and realizing who I am in Him, I was able to overcome many obstacles that were against me and strongholds that had me bound. I thank God for allowing this to be a personal testimony and to be used as a tool to help many women across the nation.

I share my testimony that not only allowed me to find God, but allowed God to set me free! Who the Son sets free is free indeed! I realized it's a part you have to play even before God is able to do His part. We tie His hands because we keep holding on to things and people who does not mean us any good. In my letting go and crying out to God, He began to remove heaviness that had me confined.

This book gave me my life back. A hunger was created in me to be better. I pray it does the same for you. You deserve to do better but it starts with you being better. You must let God work inside out.

It's like planting a seed. Imagine God planting seeds inside of you and then others seeing the fruit! Amen.

Okay this book is different from other books, because usually the exercises follow the material that has been read in its entirety. But I have an exercise I need for you to complete before you start reading this book.

Allow yourself time alone with God, so you can truly get the blessing you deserve and want.

There's no need to rush. Take your time, meditate on each question and allow the Holy Spirit to minister to you.

Remember losing weight is a process. We must learn how to remove the rush out of the process and replace rush with reach. Reach your way through the process. It takes time and discipline. You must see yourself there before your arrival.

Have faith that you will; one day at a time.

Let's begin the journey.

EXERCISE PART I

1. List the things you want to lose. Before making your list, ask God to bring those things to your remembrance. You may want to lose weight in the following categories: physical, emotional, and/or mental weight. Be honest so this can help you.

2. Make a list of things you want to be delivered from.

3. Write the things you want to be forgiven for.

4. To be forgiven we must forgive! Record the names of others that you need to forgive.

5. Write the offenses of the above names.

6. The most important step is to list the things you need to forgive yourself for.

The purpose of each assignment is for the following:
You must recognize what and/or who you're carrying in order for you to begin the separation.

Deliverance must take place for you to be set free.

You know better than anyone what things you have done wrong publicly and secretly, so only you can confess your sins and ask to be forgiven of them.

Also, those things people have done to hurt you that you may or may not discuss, but it is still doing its damage. Listing their names helps you forgive them, but writing their offenses helps you overcome the offense; so no one can repeat it again. If the offense is repeated, it can no longer hurt you.

I encourage you to focus on forgiving yourself. In so many cases people and God has forgiven us, but we are still unforgiving toward ourselves and we can't be free!

I am sure this assignment was not easy for you, but you will be happy you did it! Well, I'm not going to hold you any longer, so get on your mark, get set, And Go!

WEIGHT LOSS
CHAPTER I

WALKING WITH WEIGHT
Overweight

Weight – Heaviness, a measure of heaviness, burden or pressure: The weight of responsibility; importance or consequence. Heavy object used for exercise; an object to hold something down, to make heavy; to oppress or burden.

How many of you want to lose weight? You are weighed down and tired of carrying around those extra pounds. I know you think I am talking about physical weight gain by eating too much and over indulging in food, but not this time. What I am talking about is the emotional and mental weight gain. The weight that has you exhausted and fatigue keeps you waking up various times of the night because your spirit is overweight. You have a ton of bricks on both sides of your shoulders. It has you with migraines and you wish you could lose this pressure. Is there anyone who knows what I am talking about?

I was once there and I am here to share my story with you, so the next time I see you; you will be weightless. So let's take a moment to thank God, in advance, for the shedding of pounds that we are going to lose right here right now!

Lord, I thank you right now for the word reaching every woman that is overweight with worldly issues.

I pray she will lose weight instantly after hearing this message, you have instilled in me.

I thank you for allowing me to be able to shed more pounds by bringing this Word forth. In Jesus' Name Amen!

MIRROR THERAPY

Have you looked in the mirror lately? Do you feel mirrors tell the truth? Or do you believe they lie? Well, consider it this way. A mirror tells the truth about your outer appearance, not your inner demeanor. It can't express who you are. You are able to dress up your hurt and pain in a mirror. You can tell the mirror that you are okay today, because you appear that way in the mirror. Are you really okay?

Let's do a quick exercise. Stand in front of the mirror. What or who do you see? Do you detect any insecurities, abandonment, molestation of any kind, fear, doubt, grief, confusion, anger, jealousy, or anything else you might be dealing with?

Now go to a friend or a love one, ask them to be your mirror and ask them what do they see? Before they answer the question, be sure they understood the question. We did not ask *how you look*. The question was what do they see? Were they honest? Yes, about what they observed on the outside, but not on the inside? We are given many opportunities to help others by telling them the truth, but instead we choose to photo shop them by hiding their blemishes. I challenge you from this day forward not to hide them; but treat them.

If you glance in the mirror and notice a pimple on your face, what's the first thing you're going do?

The first thing a woman does is reach for her makeup. Why? Her first thought, is to hide it. Remember that you have other options; the one that is most helpful is to make an appointment to the dermatologist and get treated, so you can get rid of it for good!

Let's start with treating ourselves.

We all deal with issues of weight; so don't be ashamed because this too shall pass!

The most important thing about weight is you can lose it!

There are three forms of weight I will discuss. One form is physical weight. I'm sure you are familiar with what that consists of, because so many people these days, including children; are considered obese.

Let's define obese: **extremely overweight!**

But do not be fooled. Just because a person has a slender figure does not mean they are not overweight.

Now what if I told you there's another form of weight and it's called "emotional weight". This type of weight is invisible, but the most damaging. And it can bring forth the physical weight.

Mental weight also affects your thoughts of yourself and others. Yes, they are all connected. The good news is if you can lose one; you can lose every one of them!

So the next time you see someone overweight, please do not judge them because you have absolutely no idea what emotional and/or mental weight is connected to them. This means you do not know what they're going through or has been through.

WEIGHT GROWS IN STAGES

Weight is nourished by unhealthy complaints and discouraging words. Which helps bring tormenting thoughts. Weight grows in ounces turns into pounds. The more it grows the heavier it gets. My weight grew from my childhood into my adulthood.

I can remember waking up seeing my mother with black eyes and busted lips. She had bruises all over her body. I cried, comforted her, and told her everything was going to be alright. I was around seven or eight years of age. How many can agree that is weight for a baby girl of my age at that time? I couldn't sleep at night, play outside with my friends, or spend the night out; without worrying if he was beating on my mother?

My concentration was broken in second or third grade, because I daydreamed about my mother. I watched the clock, impatiently waiting on the bell to ring. I wanted to grab my book bag and run home from school to kiss my mother's beautiful face. Some days I found her in one piece and other days she was shattered into pieces. But I didn't mind picking the pieces up and pasting them back together. No matter what, it was worth the run to make sure she was still alive. Here's the first letter **W** in the word Weight! How many people believe everything starts at home?

My parents were very good parents to their children; but at times not so good to one another.

During my childhood, I kind of remind myself of Forest Gump, always running. I ran to or from something or someone.

Running home from school was a nightmare too, because I had to run from girls that wanted to fight me. A gang of them chased me. I never knew them and couldn't understand why they wanted to hurt me, but all I did was run. My brother laughed at me while walking but I did not care. I ran!

One day I got tired of running from them and told my best friend these girls on the next block keep chasing me. She said, "Well what do you want to do?" I explained to her I just wanted it to stop. She said, "Come on let's go take care of it." I was afraid, but I knew I was with one of the bullies so I should have been okay. We went to confront the girl, caught her alone, and began to do the shoulder fight. When I looked over my shoulder, my so-called friend had left me. And the girl's brother, a mentally challenged guy grabbed me from behind and held me while his sister bit me in my face.

Now I have to explain this to my mother. I was hurt that she bit me in my face, but more hurt because the friend that I thought had my back didn't. Be careful what you run to and who you run with! Here's the second letter **E** in the word weight.

Because I went to school out of district, I had to walk three or four miles to school every morning and home in the afternoon. I was forced to cross a four lane street with my brother. He was three years younger than I. He constantly pulled away not wanting to hold my hand and my mother threatened my life before I left every morning! "If you let my son get hit by a car, I'm going to kill you!" She exclaimed. I guess she never considered anything happening to me. Did she ever think I may get hit by a car? This was too much responsibility for me at seven years old. Here's the third letter **I** in the word weight.

I had to run from two men that were working with each other to kidnap me. I mean that sounds unreal but its real! It was a Caucasian guy that worked day shift. Yes, the Caucasian guy would wait outside my house, on the side of the church for me to walk to school every morning. He looked much like Freddy Krueger. He drove an old green pickup truck, he drove real slow asking my brother and I did we want a ride to school. I shook my head no! I began walking briskly to get away from him. He never missed a day of being there.

I guess, he got tired of trying to persuade me into coming with him and decided he would snatch me. This particular afternoon they switched up their routine. The Caucasian guy was outside of the church one afternoon when I came home from school. He jumped out of his truck and chased me. I ran into my building, but thank God the superintendent was at the door, and he let me in because I truly believe that would have been the last day my mother would have seen me.

I can remember the door shutting in his face and I was so thankful to God for not letting him catch me. I ran up two flights of stairs to be locked out of my house. I sat there in front of my door, praying my mother or my neighbors come home. My mother came home and I hugged her because I could have been snatched out of her life in an instant, but she had no clue. Here's the fourth letter **G** in the word weight.

Are you wondering did I ever tell anyone? Yes, I told both parents but they never checked into it.

These were the beginning stages of my emotional weight gained. Sad to say, I shouldn't have had to walk because my stepfather had a car. But they would be up the night before getting high, fighting, or maybe having sex all night; so they were too tired to take us to school. I dealt with the **consequences of their weight.**

I can recall one night, my stepfather asked me to go to Roy Rogers to get him a roast beef sandwich. I looked out of my third floor apartment window, across the street sat the Black Gorilla man that worked night shift to try to kidnap me. I explained to my dad the man was out there sitting on the wall. He asked, "What man?" I said, "The man that's trying to kidnap me." His response was "Girl aint no man trying to kidnap you, it's all in your head!"

Well, he made me go to the restaurant to get his sandwich but he promised he would look out of the third floor window, while I crossed the dark street and having to pass the big black gorilla. I remember it clearly.

I walked into Roy Rogers and placed the order. When I looked in the other line, there he was getting an order of fries. I was terrified! He got his fries before I got my sandwich. He threw them in the trash, went back outside, and sat on the wall waiting for me.

My mother taught me at an early age to pay attention to my inner voice; always follow my gut instinct and I did. As I went to the door to leave, I saw the monster sitting there but my stepfather was not in the window. I went back into the restaurant, ask the security guard to watch me go home because that man was going to snatch me. He guarded me while I ran home. I was running home once again! The thing that bothers me the most is, if he had snatched me, what could my father do in the window? Here's the fifth letter $\mathbf{H}$ in the word weight.

I know he was mad at me, because I would always outsmart the both of them, but truthfully God protected me and I thank Him so much! Listen to your children because it's your job to protect them. Even when it sounds untrue; check into it!

I am grateful to Mr. Joe. This was an older guy that loved my mother and when someone loves your mother they should love you. He did. One hot summer day, while riding my bike, I noticed a familiar green truck and as I continued up the street; I saw Freddy. I road my bike to the corner store of Mr. Joe's brother, because Mr. Joe would always be there sitting under the tree. I told him about the men that were working together to abduct me, he went and had a conversation with him. I never saw him again!

I thank Mr. Joe so much because I had someone to believe me and confronted him on my behalf. It was such a relief but I was still very alert and paid close attention to my surroundings, but God will always send a hero to rescue you. I thank God for using Mr. Joe; he became one of my heroes.

EYES HAVEN'T SEEN EARS HAVEN'T HEARD

There were things I just should not have seen or heard!

My step dad was a construction worker, truck driver, and a big time drug dealer. I can remember him coming in the house dirty and my mother cursed him out. She loved a clean house but he felt like, "Girl, I'm out here busting my behind every day. I allow you to sit here; you better hush and clean up after me." Now of course he added other words and maybe even created a new language but he got his point across. She made sure she got her point across as well, but he won in the end.

My father did not believe in bringing company to the house because he had daughters. So he was very careful who he brought home, but every so often he scheduled a few meetings.

His brothers came over and every time they got together he put that middle piece in the table. This extension made the table longer. He had scales, sifters, and a lot of powder on the table. Also, there were spoons and lighters. I didn't know what it was being so young, but I figured it was wrong because he chased us to the back room. My siblings and I couldn't get anything to eat, or drink unless they brought it to us, or we waited until they finished.

It was a lot that went on in our house; but even more that went on around the block. Imagine this set up. I stayed directly across the street from a church, across from the church was a restaurant, across from the restaurant was a hotel, and across from the hotel was a liquor store. Not to mention the corner store around the corner and the liquor store on practically every corner.

We lived on the third floor of our building and we had to go to the basement of the building to wash our clothes. Every now and then my mother asked me to go get the clothes or to put them in the dryer. She gave me a few quarters, told me to go to the second washer and put those clothes in the dryer. I followed instructions well so I did what she instructed. Always was proud to put a smile on her face!

One day she asked me to go to the laundry room and I walked in on a man shooting dope. I rushed back to the elevator and thank God he didn't come after me because I scared him too. But I remember blood squirting on the wall. I ran down the hall after getting off of the elevator and told my mother. She went with me but he was gone; unlike the memory it has always been there. This was not something that happened to me physically, but mentally it affected me and it allowed more fear to creep into my being. Here is the sixth letter **T** in the word weight.

So far what do we have? The weights of seeing your mother physically abused, having the responsibility of my brother and myself, being afraid of my life due to girls wanting to harm me and men wanting to kidnap me. Also, I was being exposed to drugs; all of this between the ages of seven to ten years old.

Children are not a product of what happened to them. But they are affected by their environments and the choices of their parents.

A LIFETIME VACATION

I remember my grandmother asked if we could come to Atlanta, Georgia for the summer. Well, my mother allowed us to go to the ATL with my grandmother. For the first time I experienced being free from the pressure. I still worried about my mother. I didn't want to leave her, but I was crazy about my grandmother. My mother convinced me that she would be okay, so I went.

I was so happy I didn't have to worry about those men and the girls trying to fight me anymore. Visiting Georgia liberated me. Would you believe when I came to Georgia, there was a man kidnapping and killing children? I couldn't believe it! But we had a curfew when the streetlights came on. No, actually every other child did but for our safety we went in too. I felt like I went from bad to worst!

Girls were jealous of me because I had long gorgeous hair, dimples, nice smile, and soft skin. It registered to me that I would have those problems whenever an insecure girl was around, so I paid it no mind. I was friends with a bully but she decided one day to bully me. I stood up and said not so. I ran home and when I got home we rumbled. Where I came from they jumped you. I never wanted to chance more than one girl double teaming little ole me! **Light weight**!

The summer vacation became a permanent stay for us. My grandmother tricked my mother into moving to Georgia. We were supposed to be in Georgia only for the summer vacation, but my grandmother was on trial at the time. And she needed her grandchildren to stay here to help her case. I agreed with her.

So she transferred us from school without my mother's permission. I knew something was wrong because of the lies that were being told. But children won't speak up when they feel it is beneficial to them. I guess I can take some blame, because I heard my grandmother telling the courts and the schools that my mother abandoned us. Also, she had no contact with my mother. All lies, but my mother didn't find out until she came to Atlanta to get us and realized we were already enrolled in school. We begged her to stay and so she did.

Georgia was a cleaner environment to live in, better schools and overall better quality of living than Newark, New Jersey. It is a saying that you can take the person out the ghetto, but not the ghetto out the person. I'm not saying my mother was ghetto, but I am saying the drug abuse came with her and the physical abuse followed my dad.

I must say that it got worse!

The fights with my parents and their drug addiction had gotten worst. We moved from Six Flags Drive to Martin Luther King Jr. Drive. That should be enough said. We moved from Twin Hill Townhouses to Allen Temple Apartments. We went from paying market rent, to subsidized housing apartments. Why am I saying this? We were exposed to more drugs and children were everywhere, so now more fights.

Now my grandmother, uncle, mother, and father are on drugs. I feel like we went from riches to rags. **Weight**!

A GUILTY ESCAPE

Every so often my mother allowed me to spend the night out with a close friend of mine in Austell. Every time I did, I felt guilty when I returned home because my mother had a black eye or busted lip. One time he hit her wrist with a hammer and broke it. I mean this was getting out of control!

I was happy when they broke the news. They decided to end their relationship. Finally, I saw a light in the dark valley. At least that's what I thought. I was happy for my dad to leave, because the fights stopped. But I loved him. At the time of him leaving, his children needed him the most.

Our mother dated other guys so we had to adjust to the change. As children you do not always agree but you don't have a say, so you just adapt. Kids want their mom to be happy. And mothers know that if they're not happy no one is; so whatever makes the boss happy.

I prayed that their drug abuse would stop, that my father would stop abusing my mother, my grandmother and mother one day would show each other love. I prayed our kitchen cabinets, refrigerator, and freezer were filled with food to eat every day instead of every once in a while. I prayed my siblings and I could one day wear clothes from the mall and not the thrift store. No more fly away collars or bell-bottom pants (I mean they enjoy wearing them now). Also, I prayed one day we would own a washer and dryer to wash our clothes. No longer having to do it by hand, praying the clothes are dry when we wake up in the morning. Not having to borrow bread or sugar or whatever else from our neighbors. I mean you're talking about **weight;** I had weight for you! All of this was between the ages of ten and twelve.

See if weight is not removed it builds. The weight starts to wear and tear on your physical body, stresses you out mentally, and emotionally you are out of control.

You will be carrying weight from knee high up; not knowing but adjusting! If your back hurts, you may switch positions to get comfortable but the pressure is still there.

Well, I'm going to share just a little more about my childhood weight so we can get right into the heavy weights. Do you know even with the lighter weights, if it's too many at one time they are too heavy?

Imagine coming home from school and your furniture is on the side of the street. And your friend laughed at you because you were evicted from your apartment. Did I say friend? Yes, I did. My brother's friend seen me walking home from school and he laughed at me. He said, "Y'all got put out!" I said, "No sir, you got the wrong family!" Because I am sure our rent is paid. Well, truthfully my mother's boyfriend, a drug dealer without any drug addictions of any sort would have paid the rent.

I wasn't aware that he gave my mother the money twice to pay the rent and she smoked it up. She had a plan though. She knew she would get her AFDC check and sell a few food stamps to pay the rent, but someone stole the check. I mean, when you think things are getting better they only seem to get worse! This guy was determined to prove to me that we got put out, so he walked with me about three miles to show me. After passing several families, with the last family being mine, I must say, it was heart breaking seeing my mother's face knowing we had been evicted.

When she saw me she began to curse me out and I was so confused, but now I understand her. That had to be the hardest thing for her. To look your daughter in her face knowing, that you're the cause of her being in the streets. She cried and I walked away with my head down in tears. **More weight!**

With my mother not having a trusting relationship with her mother, she put our furniture in this lady's house she didn't even know. The lady didn't have any furniture. We went to her house every week to change out our clothes and one day a friend of mine went with me.

When we got to the door of the apartment while knocking, I realized the knob was off of the apartment door. I looked into the hole of the door and there was nothing in the house.

Can you believe this lady moved out with our furniture, clothes, trophies, and family portraits? I mean, she took our life with her! And I had to be the one to bare the news with my dear mother. **Weight on top of weight!**

This is when we began going pillow to post.

Now we're the talk of the town. My mother gets strung out even more on drugs, because she feels she has nothing to live for. How many knows that sometimes it gets worse before getting better?

Whatever you do, don't give up faith and continue to pray. That's exactly what I did! Yes, it was hard when you see things getting worse. But God hears you and He will show up on time!

My brother and sister stayed with my grandmother and I went from one friend's house to the next. I probably should have stayed with my grandmother. But she fused and cursed us too much so I refused to be with her!

Mother was living from place to place and hotel to hotel. I moved with a friend the day my family got put out. I met this young lady the same day I got evicted. Her mother accepted me into her home. It was different from the way I was used to living, but beggars don't complain.

My friend was sexually active and her mother called us the B word. It bothered me so much. I remember asking her "Why does she call me out of my name?" When I told her I was a virgin she responded by saying, "Well you need to be careful who you befriend." That was a strong statement coming from her when it's her daughter who I befriended. Regardless, she is my buddy and I know who I am.

I moved with a friend of mine in Austell, Georgia. Her father owned a liquor store; he allowed my mother to work there and paid her every week. He never asked her for any money to help support me. He clothed me, gave me shelter, and basically took care of me as if I was his own. See every now and then God knows the pressure builds up so He will allow the steam to be released. Reminds me much of a teapot. He used my friend's family to relieve me. My mother knew I was safe there and she didn't have to worry.

I was in a safe place but I always prayed for my mother to get herself together. Because I realized no matter where you live, if it's not with your family; you always feel something is missing. And it will make you incomplete within. I mean I had everything, a nice home, food, nice clothing, and was able to go places like six flags. Still there's no place like home!

Nothing lasts forever. I can remember waking up and seeing her brothers standing over me. I told her, she told her parents, and they both were punished. A few weeks later, one of them decided to put my breast in his mouth and sucked it, while I was asleep.

When I woke up I was in shock! I couldn't believe he did this to me. Yes, his parents decided that I needed to leave, but it was other things I had done to help them make this decision. Against their wishes, I accepted collect phone calls on their phone when they told me not to. **The pressure is building up again at this point!**

I ended up going back to Atlanta staying with another friend. These households were in two total different areas, ran totally different, but they both took me in without questioning it. I had an opportunity to move with my teacher and her family. But I felt after dealing with the situation with the brother it wouldn't be wise to do so, because she was married. **Adjusting again!**

The pressure of being separated from your mother and siblings, a guy that I looked at like as my brother has violated me, going from one house to the next, and I was still being faced with the fact that what I prayed for has not changed. I wondered will it ever change. Lord, Please **Remove The Weight!**

I found myself wanting to die and always asking God, "Why me?" I never heard Him speak back, so now I have more questions. Does God exist? Does God love me? If so, why won't He stop all of this confusion? They say He has all powers and can do whatever He wants so why God… why?

Whatever you do, just continue to pray! Pray without ceasing! Your breakthrough will soon come. Thank you Jesus…

A Child's Mentality

At age thirteen, I decided to give up my virginity. I thought my mother would probably die on drugs and I wanted someone that no one can take from me. I soon became pregnant at fourteen and my mother went into treatment thirty days before finding out I was pregnant. I gave out when she gave in! The word says, *"Don't grow weary in well doing, for in due season we shall reap if you faint not."* I grew weary but my mother got clean.

I became a teenage mother at fifteen, a high school dropout at seventeen, and a welfare recipient at eighteen. I was abused verbally and physically by my boyfriend from fifteen until eighteen. The abortion table called me seven months after my first born. Third child but second born at age seventeen. I reversed what my mother did to me onto her. I added weight on her plate, at a time she was removing weights of her own. I was going down a downward spiral. But think of it this way; when you are weighed down you will go down.

They say the sky is the limit but only if you're going in the upward direction. If you're headed downward your bottom is the limit!

It was one thing after another. My daughter's father got arrested and sentenced fourteen years. She was only five at the time. A teenager left to raise a baby alone, thinking she was grown. The only knowledge I had of raising children would have been feeding and clothing them. Never realizing it was so much more! My friends taught me to look forward to having a baby so I can get welfare, food stamps, and an apartment based on my income. I did exactly that and fell into statistics.

I went from one relationship to the next, trying to find love, and looking for someone to love me the way I wanted to be loved. I was never able to carry out either one successfully.
I dealt with so much trying to raise kids, work, and have a relationship.

Not to mention, having to go to school and trying to fit in with my friends. The whole time I was hurting and crying inside, wanting someone to stop the bleeding while not being able to pinpoint the wounds. I bled from so many areas and it took more than a bandage to stop the bleeding, it took much more than that. Sometimes the wound gets infected and has to get reopened, cleaned and re-bandaged so it can heal properly.

Which reminds me of when I had my first C-Section, and my incision got infected. When I went to the doctor he took a q-tip and reopened the cut. Let me tell you that was one of my most painful experiences! He did not warn me at all! He cleaned and stuffed it with gauge. He gave me the same cleaning solution and plenty of gauges; He instructed me to clean the incision three times a day. I was terrified! I said, "Doctor you're not going to stitch it back up?" He replied, "No sweetheart it has to heal inside out, so be sure not to do a lot of bending, lifting, and/or walking upstairs." Wow! What a revelation through that situation.

I went home and explained everything to my mother. She started off cleaning it but after two times she said that she could not continue to do so, her stomach was too weak. I was either going to learn how to do this alone and heal properly or whine for my mother to do it and not heal.

There are scars that mommy or daddy won't be able to heal but God! Even with Jesus help, He wants you to play a part in your healing. Do you understand where I am going with this?

Many times the wound forms a scab, the wound looks healed so we start picking at the scab and it reopens to bleed again. We are the same way with our healing. We must allow time for the healing method to take place.

THE HEALING METHOD:

1. To properly cleanse the wound.

2. It must be covered securely.

3. Removal of the bandage in a timely manner.

4. Allow air to get to the wound.

5. Do not pick at the scab; let it fall off on its own.

6. It might leave a scar after it's completely healed but don't disregard it. It's only a reminder.

7. Now old school says put some cocoa butter on it so the scar can disappear.

8. They say when it itches that's a sign of it healing.
9. As I explained earlier, in some cases, the wound must me re-opened!

How can I relate this with our healing process? Glad you're wondering so let me explain.

1. We have to go through a cleansing process.
2. Then God will cover us so we can heal properly.
3. Eventually we are exposed because He has to show the world we're overcomers.
4. He will breathe fresh Air and Anointing in us and on us!
5. Stop going back to what you were delivered from; picking at the devil.
6. The scar is a reminder to protect you from any future falls!
7. The Oil is always good. Once God saturates you in the Holy Spirit you will no longer be reminded, because the Holy Spirit reminds them! Amen.

8. You're itching to go back, but that is exactly when you're at your best! Healing is taking place.

Right now just pray and thank God for Chapter I, because having to go back and reopen those covered but infected wounds was not easy but worth it. You are on your way to a Better You with a Better Future!

Let's recap Chapter I

1. Let go and give whatever is weighing you down, to God.

2. Pray and ask God for His forgiveness, forgive others, and more importantly forgive yourself.

3. Repent daily!

4. Pray and push! Pray without ceasing.

5. Stop complaining! What you focus on you give power to so focus on the positive. That leaves you no room to complain.

6. Do not turn the weight that can be removed into a long waiting process.

WEIGHT LOSS
CHAPTER II

WEIGHTLESS
Detox

Weightless – Having or experience little or no heaviness. Free from the pull of gravity, as in outer space.

I received a phone call from a friend and he shared with me Dr. Oz's weight loss program. I began to listen, because I was interested in losing weight. I tried several times with friends, but half of the time it was to support them. I didn't look like what I actually weighed. That is how the devil deceived me. This time it was for me so he continued to share. After hanging up with him, I asked my son to take pictures of the front, back, and sides of me. I'm a visual person so I need to see what I'm working on, so that I can detect the difference. After I looked at my picture of the rear of me, I began to cry. I cried out to God for help because I could not do this alone.

The more I looked at the picture I visualized something:

I challenge you to take a moment and visualize with me. Have you ever been somewhere and a heavyset lady walks in the door and you say, "OMG! How did she let herself get there?" Well, I began to see myself as that woman and asked God how did I get here?

He gave me a couple of things:

1. I lost myself

2. I put everyone before me

3. I do not invest in myself

4. I stopped loving myself

As you can see after the four above sentences, I refuse to put a period. Why? It's not the end! Amen. If you are experiencing one or more of the above just know this is not the end so DO NOT PUT A PERIOD!

LOOK ALIKE

I used to wear hand me down clothes, all of my friends gave me what they didn't want or could not fit anymore. Now don't get me wrong there is nothing wrong with getting used clothes, because someone may need them. But as for me, I sacrificed for my man, my children, my friends, but never for myself.

It got so bad; I started looking like the people who gave me the garments. I lost my sex appeal. I didn't even know when I looked good in anymore. I wore people's clothes since I was twelve years old and it didn't stop until I was thirty-five years old. I really had no clue of my style anymore! See how what started in my childhood, followed me into my adulthood, or shall I say I carried it with me all this time.

God's Mercy

I'm blessed to not have had a stroke, heart attack, ulcers, tumors and any other illness that comes from worrying. I was carrying things for twenty-four years or better. I carried people and their problems too.

We are not created to carry weight! We must begin to think of our physical health, because we can start accumulating stress and health issues that God did not intend on us carrying.

Majority of our health issues comes from worrying! We begin to worry, then we neglect our responsibility of caring for ourselves and overtime we become diabetics, diagnosed with high blood pressure, and heart problems.

God is merciful! He continues to show compassion and forgives us because He knows we do not know what we do. That is why I am here making you aware so we do not continue to put ourselves at risk in this manner anymore.

DELIVERIES

Now how much weight are you going to continue to haul on your back? Do you think you are a tow truck? Even tow trucks make deliveries to the owners, car repair shops, or the junkyard. We must learn to do the same.

When you call for a tow truck to pick up your car after it breaks down, what's the first thing that they ask? What's your AAA number, location, and are you safe? If I can be truthful, I believe they ask those particular questions for them. What do you mean Kisha? They want to be sure you can pay for the service. Also, making sure they are not sending their workers to a dangerous situation.

When they arrive, their only concern is what's the address to the destination to drop off the vehicle? If you do not have a location for them, they will give you an address to where they're going to drop it off. What? Yes, they have enough sense to know they are not going to tow your vehicle around, keeping them from being able to make money.

We have to get to a point where we help people make the deliveries properly. If you go to a friend house that has been carrying too much, assist them with the following:

1. Allow them to vent. Yes, this is the way you began to get the car on the tow truck.

2. Then touch and agree with them. This is the towing process. Taking it off of them, not allowing them to be weighed down anymore but not allowing you to pick it up either.

3. Now we will send it to our Lord Jesus Christ! It's His to carry not ours.

You are not a tow truck or a junkyard, so stop pretending you are! You are a human being that can only handle but so much. The Lord said, "He won't put more on you than you can bear." So do yourself and others a favor and Stop It by dropping it!

The Lord said, "Cast all your cares upon Him." So please tell me why you're hauling all of that junk?

Let it go!

FEEDING THE VOID

God showed me I was an emotional eater. Emotional people eat when they're happy, sad, or even excited. Well, I ate off of every emotion. I ate when I was happy, sad, anxious, and off of every other emotion. I ate whatever I wanted, how much of it I wanted, and whatever time I wanted to eat it (2am a pan of cookies out the oven). Sounds good to me how about you?

If you don't love yourself how do you expect anyone else to?

Are you always comparing yourself with others? If they are doing better than you, you feel bad; if they're doing worse, you feel good. We have to get to a point where we are not comparing ourselves to anyone.

Think about this, to compare is to compete! If I compare myself to someone, I'm sizing them up. And now I'm going to compete to be like them, but that is NOT the answer.

You have to be yourself and learn to love yourself, right now where you are; the way you are!

When you start to love yourself, you will become concerned about your appearance, you will stop settling, and start sacrificing for yourself.

I did not love myself and I was searching for others to love me. But the void I felt, I began to feed it with food. Food cannot feed the void of love, compassion, and/or companionship!

MY DETOXIFICATION BEGINS

My step dad came down south every Thanksgiving from New Jersey to visit us after my mother passed away. Every time he came my hair was pulled back into a ponytail and I had on a jogging suit. Well, he talked about it the entire time he was here. "Why won't you do something with your hair? Get dressed? Go out and do something with yourself? Stop acting like an old lady!" I got so sick and tired of hearing it but never tired enough to make me do something different.

My grandmother, uncle, friends, and even my children said this and I ignored them. I don't have any money to do those things; I must pay bills! I'm sure you're saying, "I know that's right!" Chile please, you better see about yourself! Not sure which one you're saying, but I couldn't afford to spend money foolishly. Is buying yourself some clothes really being foolish? No not at all!

My grandmother gave me two hundred dollars for Christmas and she said that she wanted me to go and buy myself some new clothes. Before my thought was complete, she finished it by saying, "I know all you're going to do is spend it on a bill." I was thinking to myself, "You got that right sweetie." God spoke to me and said, "No you're not! You are going to do exactly what she says." I was like, yes sir! So I guess, I'll go put this money in the bank, because I'm not going against what my daddy says. I put the money in the bank and the money sat in the bank for two months.

I did not rush to spend it because I was determined to lose weight before buying any new clothes. I planned this not God.

WOMAN TO WOMAN

My aunt flew from New Jersey for Christmas and New Year's. Around the third day of her being here she said, "Why won't you do something with your hair? Dress up? Go out?" She sounds like a broken record huh? Sounds like my dad too. Yes, but believe it or not this time it started working on me. Women relate with women.

In the months of November and December God spoke to me and He said, "I want to take you places, but I can't if you don't leave your poverty state of mind." I felt bad and a little offended; because I didn't know my thoughts were in a poverty state. God doesn't speak about your emotions; He speaks the truth! The truth was I had a poverty way of thinking. Yes, I did!

My aunt is fifty years old and looks every bit of thirty; I'm not exaggerating at all. This woman looks better than half of the younger ladies including myself. When I say her hair was flawless, eyebrows arched, nails and toes done, and has a beautiful figure. She can dance and loves to have fun. Her spirit is so uplifting and that is exactly what God allowed her to do with me, lift my spirits. Thank you Jesus!

My aunt uplifted my spirits. I told her I would do my hair if I had a beveling iron and a blow dryer. She and I went to the store to get me one. I was going to purchase it, but instead my aunt did. God allowed her to buy it, so it would put pressure on me to keep my promise to her. I vowed to her I would keep my hair looking nice, eyebrows arched, and my toes done. I kept my promise since December 30, 2009.

During the summer it's been extremely hard because of the heat and I don't have a working air conditioner in my car. So my hair continues to sweat out. Also, my funds are low, so I'm not able to keep my eyebrows and feet done as much as I want, but from time to time I make the sacrifice. It's not only about the outer appearance though.

HE KNOWS THE PLANS

I attended service one Saturday morning, my Bishop's wife (Dr. Nina Bronner) was preaching to the women. It was right after my aunt went back home. After service I went to Dillard's to pay my bill. While driving there the Holy Spirit said, "Stop by the bank and withdraw that two hundred dollars." I'm like huh? But I haven't lost weight yet. I did withdraw the money and I remembered I received a coupon for New York & Company. I went to make a payment on my account and then headed to NY&C.

I went in the store, the first thing I picked up were three pants brown, blue, and black. I put them aside, kept looking around and I couldn't find anything else. I was in this store for five hours; Mrs. Angel came by and asked did I need help. I said, "Yes, I do need help." I explained to her that I didn't have any clothes and I wanted to start building my wardrobe. I told her I am tired of wearing hand me downs!

I was honest with this lady. I told her I did not know what makes me appealing anymore. I am struggling! I am a very honest person and in this case, I had to be truthful with her in order for her to be able to help me. Many of us want help and need help, but when help come we are too ashamed to share where we are. Or we allow our pride to get in the way!

Do you realize if you do not give a person the full details, they won't be able to help you? So I made sure she knew I did not have any clothes and I am tired of wearing everyone else's clothing. I was becoming a duplicate when I am created to be an original! I wanted a new look and to be made brand new!

God knows His plans for you…

PLANS TO PROSPER YOU

Before she came to me I kept going back and forth from the clearance rack and God said, "Didn't I tell you to leave your poverty state of mind." Again nothing is wrong with the clearance rack but God is doing something in me. He is trying to show me it's my time and don't be concerned about the price, get what you want. Your daddy is taking you shopping today; it's my treat. Amen!

She said, "Not a problem; I can help!" She started putting these different outfits together, variety of colors and styles I wouldn't have dreamed of wearing. I went in the dressing room, I tried them on and I liked them. My concern was my mid area (stomach). Angel said, "What's wrong my dear?" I nodded my head nothing. She said, "It's your stomach right? But I have something for that." I wondered how does she know, but I checked out with six outfits and a belt and I was proud!

Angel directed me back to Dillard's to pick up a Spanx. She instructed me to get that particular brand to help me hold my stomach in and to smooth my mid area underneath my clothing. I went there expeditiously!

I arrived at Dillard's and a young lady by the name of Ms. Special helped me. First, I asked her to size me for a bra, because I had recently purchased me a size 38 DD and it appeared that I had a third breast. She sized me and said that I needed a 38 DDD. Look at how the devil began trying to torment me, because he knew my deliverance was close. I didn't get discouraged. So I said, "Go get it!" Before she left to go, I asked her to bring me a spanx. She said, "Not sure if we have it because we don't get many. But I will check for you, what's your size?" I am clueless to my size, but she came back with the last one, a large. Yes, I WAS SMILING! And to my surprise, it was my size.

Bishop Bronner preached Thursday on the right timing, a Kairos moment and yes, I was experiencing just that! Amen...

Everything fell into place. I didn't have to do anything, but follow God's lead. I encourage you to allow your daddy to take you shopping one day, I enjoyed my shopping spree!

Well, Ms. Special came in the dressing room, she put the bra on me, I began to cry and she cried with me. She said, "I have never seen anyone so excited over a bra." I was full because I literally stood straight up when she put it on me. I couldn't believe it. Then, I put the spanx on and my new outfit to see the finished product. I smiled and screamed, "Look at me!" I looked so good and felt great. You will be surprised with the change that under garments and wearing the right size garments will bring to your body.

God spoke to me at that moment and said, "You must look good during the process!"

You have to love yourself right here, where you are. Love yourself in this moment, right now. I received what He said and it's been uphill from that moment and the weight has gone downhill.

I came home and I had a fashion show for my children. They cheered me on and told me how good I looked! I started hanging up my clothes. I even bought jewelry to wear with my outfits, a belt, and the only thing left to buy were shoes.

I went to Off Broadway and DSW to buy my shoes. A sister has been on point from that moment. I have had days when I didn't dress up but I still felt good within myself. God's main concern is your internal look.

When I looked into my closet at those six outfits, I felt I had a closet full of clothes. I was like a student just going shopping for back to school clothes. And anxious to put them on in the morning, I tried them on over and over again. This boosted my spirits tremendously!

I GOT IT

People told me over and over again in the past, but when I got it, change took place. I wanted it so bad and I knew I had to change my eating habits. I'm sure many people want to lose physical weight too. I am going to share with you what worked for me. Now I can't say this will work for you, but I guarantee you it worked for my fourteen year old son that was a size 38 men pant and now is a 34 men pant. He lost it in four months. I was a size 12 and now I am a size 8. I lost the weight in four months too. We have been maintaining during the summer months, but I look forward to shedding more and get toned soon.

Now we are finally where you want to be. Tell me how to lose the physical weight! I am, but seriously speaking you needed that first because it all works together. I am so proud of your progress. I know you may feel you have not accomplished anything yet, but not so, inhale and exhale. Great job!

We have one more major part to cover. Join me in on twenty – one day fast! Yes, I said fast but we are going to refrain from negative thinking. That should be fun huh? How can I stop myself from having negative thoughts? It can be challenging but it starts by not entertaining the negative thoughts.

Do you ever question yourself? Why am I thinking this? We won't share some of our thoughts with others, because we cannot understand why we have them. Don't try to figure it out. Let's work them out (out of your brain).

Below are a few steps that were extremely helpful to me:
  Get around positive people!
  Think positive thoughts toward yourself and others.
  Choose to find the positive out of every negative situation.
The word of God says, *"The good and the bad work together for the good of those who love the Lord and to whom are called according to His purpose."*

What the devil meant for your bad; God will turn around for your good.
· Purchase positive empowering books that can feed your Spirit.
· Speak positively toward yourself and others.
· Create a positive atmosphere everywhere you go.
· You can be positive, you will be positive because you are positive.

Now it's time for us to learn to discipline this flesh. So come on turn to the next page. You heard me, turn the page!

PHYSICAL WEIGHT LOSS

Please do not flip to this page before reading the prior contents. Take your time to read the entire book because everything helped me to lose weight physically. It wasn't just one thing!

Step I – Cry out to God, ask Him to take away the stress and worrying. It's okay to be concerned but not to worry. Turn your worrying into praying!

Step II – Love yourself right where you are! Embrace yourself, fall in love with yourself, and celebrate yourself. If you don't, who else will? Look in the mirror daily and say you love yourself! Respect your body; it's The Lord's Temple.

Step III – Visual is always good for me. So take a picture of yourself, the front, sides, and the rear of your body. Look at the pictures and ask God how did you get here? I cried after seeing my picture but it was okay because it motivated me to stay persistent.

Step IV – Buy the following items: measuring tape (to measure your neck, arms, breast, waist, buttocks, thighs, legs, and ankles), and a scale to weigh yourself (but weigh yourself only in the mornings). You can weigh yourself as much as you like just don't get discouraged if the weight fluctuate. This will happen but stick with it.

Step V – Let's discuss minor adjustments. Everyone has different eating habits and weaknesses for food so that means you have to figure this out yourself.

Example: I never drunk water, always drunk Pepsi sodas, ate plenty of Kit Kats and Reese cups during that time of the month, a pan of cookies straight out of the oven at 2am. You name it I did it. So I added water, fruits, and vegetables. And I subtracted the sodas, the chocolate chips cookies, and breads.

Step VI – You must close the kitchen at 7:30pm. If you're hungry eat a yogurt or applesauce, drink water, exercise, or go to sleep.

Step VII – Downsize from a plate to a saucer. Yes, I got that from Dr. Oz. Eat breakfast! Do not skip meals especially breakfast.

Step VIII – Eat every three hours. Sounds like a lot of eating but you're eating smaller portions. As long as your body knows you will feed it, your body will release the fat. If not, fat will be stored to feed itself.

Step VIIII – Try to cut back on your salt and sugar intake. Everything you eat turns into sugar so please limit your sugar intake. Try using brown sugar in your food. It tastes great in my oatmeal.

Eat whatever you want, just do not over indulge. Too much of anything cannot be good for you.

Step X – Weigh yourself the first day you start and do your measurements once or twice a month.

Step XI – Please get a diary to keep track of your weight loss and measurements. Record your feelings daily.

Last but not least exercise is good but not mandatory! You will lose weight regardless but exercising will tone your body as you go.

* IMPORTANT!!! PURCHASE A SPANX!

It resembles a girdle but I love this brand and please get your proper size bra. Yes, that means you must be properly fitted.

So ladies… hug yourself , love on yourself, and be comfortable being yourself!

CONTINUATION OF CHAPTER II

WEIGHTLESS
Removal of Weights

Someone walked up to me and said, "You look so good! Have you lost weight?"

This was the second person in one week that asked me this question. When the second person said it I said, "Maybe I should weigh myself." My daughter got sick, I rushed her to the emergency room and I got on the scale to get weighed. No, I had not lost weight; I gained weight. I weighed one hundred and eighty five pounds strong! I was sad because I hoped I had lost weight, but I should have known. My eating habits stayed the same.

Well, I attended Sunday school. After class a young lady walked up while I was walking to the sanctuary and she said, "I remember you, you look so good! Have you lost weight?" I said, "No and you're the third person that has said this to me. I am one hundred and eighty five pounds." She said, "You look good!"

I felt good just off of her telling me how good I looked.

I was leaving church and I was sitting in the car, in heavy traffic and gas tank on E. God spoke to me and said, "Yes, you have lost weight and plenty of baggage." You are overcoming, the weight has been lifted. I received it in Jesus' Name. Amen!

I love the way my Father communicates with me, he talks to me in ways that I can understand Him. **In all things, get understanding!** I had prayed to God asking Him to let the external become a reflection of the internal.

I knew the works He had done on the inside of me, but I wanted His people to see the works. It was confirmed then in my spirit they are. **I give Him the Glory!**

I was walking around with garbage from old relationships, low self - esteem, beating myself up with past mistakes, children issues, no job, no money, the bills are overdue, and just so much made me fat and overweight. But when God started taking things off, one by one, and releasing strongholds that had me bound for years, I lost weight.

I am here to say to those that have been over-weighed emotionally, "Today you can **let go and give it to God**. This does not happen overnight, but stay strong, hold on to God, and let go of the extra stuff."

Pray and ask God His for forgiveness, to help you to forgive, for the other party to forgive you, and for you to forgive yourself. And repent!

Just give it to God. When I say give it to him, I mean let it go! Do not wrestle with trying to be heard, keeping control, and having the last word. Release it!

Pray for others and yourself. And watch as you step into His Victory! Pray and Push!

In our weakness we qualify for His strength!

YOU DECIDE

Pray until something happens. Do not curse the storm or keep complaining about the storm. Get off of the telephone discussing the storm. "Girl he gets on my nerve, I can't wait until she's grown and out of my house." Because then you are turning the Weight God can remove; to the Wait you are creating.

WAIT = time waiting
WEIGHT = pounds weigh

I do not want to make my wait any longer than it has to be, but that is what complaining and sobbing does. It is like waiting in traffic, cursing and fusing makes your wait seem even longer.

Now when you put Bishop Bronner's CD in and listen to him or turn to 102.5 (gospel station), before you know it you're at your destination and you did not realize the traffic has passed. **The only wait I want is to wait on the Lord Our God!**

Instead of getting on the phone and talking about it in a negative way, call up your prayer partner and say let's pray. Or get into your prayer closet and pray for yourself. I dare you to praise Him anyhow! Praise Him right in the situation that you are in and watch God remove you or make you fireproof. He is saying, "Look at my child carrying that luggage. All she has to do is ask me for help, but **she have not because she asks not.**"

He said, *"I am here, I am aware of everything she has done. But does she know* ***nothing can separate her from the love of God."***

If you have tons of weight, you are tired and you need the Lord to remove it; I ask you to stand. Bring your luggage to the altar. Let's touch and agree because ***where two or more come together God is in the midst!***

He is in the room. So if you knew Jesus is in the place and all you had to do was **touch the hem of His garment,** then make your way to the altar. Because **He is waiting on you to remove the Weights!**

ALTAR CALL

You're saying, "Well, I don't have an altar." Build one right there in your home. Fall on your knees in that resting, sacred place and on Holy ground. I mean my altar is wherever I pray and cry out to God! My altar is my closet, car, kitchen, and even in the front of my fireplace. Build your altar today!

Anoint yourself, prophesy over yourself and speak the word of God over your life, because His word will never return to Him void! Amen.

CREMATION/BURIAL

I **want you** to take those lists that you created in the beginning, shred it, light it up, and/or rip it up in a thousand pieces. While you are doing this, pray and ask God to release you of everything that has had you bound. Ask Him to set you free right now in the name of Jesus!

I burned my list of papers in the fireplace because I wanted to cremate them, but did not want the remembrance of keeping the ashes. My mother was cremated and I have her ashes, this is valuable to me. Yes, she is deceased, her Spirit is with our Lord and Savior, but her urn sits in my dining room. Whenever I look at it, it brings back memories. So why would I have wanted to hold on to those ashes?

The only reason I can think of, is to remind myself it is dead. With that being said, I decided to create a document so you can have a reminder of the death date of your pain and/or weight that you once carried.

Father God, we uplift you. We magnify, glorify, and honor you! You are so good to us. We thank you for everything you have in store for us. We promise we won't go back and pick up past hurt, regrets, or anything behind us. We won't allow anyone to remind us of our past not even ourselves. **You've buried them in the depths of the Sea** so we will leave them there. I touch and agree right now with the individual that you will make their **crooked ways straight**. **They are the head and not the tail, above and not beneath.**

Lord, you are BIGGER than their problem. **They are lenders and not borrowers.** With you before them; who can be against them? **We know that they can do all things through Christ Jesus who strengthens them. Your strength is made perfect in their weakness.** We qualify for your strength when we're weak, so God I thank you in advance for making them **WHOLE and COMPLETE** in you. Breaking and mending them in **Jesus' name Amen!**

Thank you Lord God Amen!
Glory to God! He is Worthy of all our Praise! Just praise Him in your own way.

Before you go to Chapter III sign and date this document. Basically, for you to always come back and be reminded that you are free from baggage. This is where you drew the line, the buck stopped here.

I vow to myself and to God I have given Him everything and I am delivered of anything and all things that are not of Him, In Jesus' Name Amen!

NAME: _____

DATE: _____

TIME: _____

We go through different phases during the weight loss process. First, we went through the process of losing emotional and mental weight. Letting go of things, people, and just overall stop the worrying about situations we had no control over. We turned things over to Jesus!

Then we were able to move to the next level; loving ourselves right where we were. We embraced our bodies with the extra rolls and all.

This is body weight I am speaking of because the emotional and mental baggage is gone. We gave that to Jesus! Amen.

God said that He won't put more on us than we can bear, right? This brings us to Weight-Loss Part III Titled: *Weight Training!*

WEIGHT LOSS
CHAPTER III

<u>WEIGHT TRAINING</u>
Shape & Strengthening

Overcome – Defeat. Prevail over. To Win!

We have to go through training to be able to endure. We do not even know our endurance level until we go through this process. Weight training is to tone and/or build muscle.

You will go through a burning process! The burning process hurts. You feel like you can't do it, it's too hard, and/or it's too many weights. You're begging for the trainer to lighten your load. **That's God! He's the trainer** and He wants to show us *we can do all things through Christ Jesus who strengthens us!* Let me say that again... *we can do all things through Christ Jesus who strengthens us!* The word says, *"His strength is made perfect in our weakness."*

This isn't baggage training because He said, *"Cast all your cares upon Him."* God doesn't train us to carry baggage; He trains us to lift weights. The more you lift the more you can tolerate. The more you can tolerate, the harder it is for you to break. Are you with me?

The trainer will put the weights on the bar; you will look up and think you can't lift it. But after a couple of times, you will be lifting more.

Will you bend while in weight training? Of course, bending is before lifting. Do your arms bend while lifting weights? Yes, God will train us to bend, but not break.

The very thing that's burning you; will no longer be able to hurt you because you're getting stronger! You're asking the trainer to please stop adding the weights, but He knows the more He adds the stronger you're getting. In conclusion, the lighter you'll become because you're toning the fat. How many know muscle weighs more than fat?
If it weighs more, it's safe to say it's stronger.

The problems you are dealing with are only weights. You can lift them up to God in prayer. Those who need to lift the bills, children, friends, and enemies; stand and pray with me. Weight lifting requires you to Praise/Pray/Read/Intercede/Believe/Focus on The LORD!

Yes, praise God regardless of your circumstances or situations. Continue to pray at all times, in the good and bad times. Read to strengthen your faith in God! Intercession is great because praying for others, always made me pray when I was not able to pray for myself. You must believe things will change! Keep your focus at all times! Whatever you focus on is what you give power to so focus on the "Most High" God. He has all of your answers!

Seek ye first the Kingdom of God and all of His righteousness and everything else will be added! Trust Him at all times.

He knows the plans He has for you; plans to prosper you not harm you.

As you know everything has a beginning and ending date. Nothing stays the same.

His anger lasts for a moment, but his favor lasts a lifetime! Weeping may endure for a night **but joy comes in the morning. Psalm 30:5.**

It will be like a woman experiencing pains of labor. When her child is born, her anguish gives place to joy because she has brought a new person in the world. *You have sorrow now, but I will see you again. Then you will rejoice and no one can rob you of that joy. At the time you won't need to ask me for anything.*

The truth is, you can go directly to the Father and ask Him and He will grant your request, because you use my name. You haven't done this before. *Ask, using my name, and you will receive, and you will have abundant joy. John 16:21-24.*

YOU GOT THE VICTORY

Victor: Winner, champion, and conqueror.
Victory: Triumph, conquest, success, and achievement.
Victorious: Triumphant and Successful.

Victory: One who wins a struggle!

Womenlations! You have successfully completed your one on one personal weight-loss training, life changing, revolutionizing emotionally, mentally, physically, and spiritually!

I AM... I CAN... I WILL...

The diary of a healthy Queen!
Below is my start to finish progress report.
I hope this encourage you.

DATE	1/19/10		DATE	8/15/13
WEIGHT	189LBS		WEIGHT	155LBS

MEASUREMENTS			*MEASUREMENTS*	
NECK	14 1/2		NECK	13
ARMS	14		ARMS	13
BUST	44		BUST	40
WAIST	40		WAIST	34
BUTT	43		BUTT	40
THIGHS	26 1/2		THIGHS	22 1/2
LEGS	15		LEGS	13
ANKLES	8		ANKLES	8
SIZE	12		SIZE	6

**Total amount of weight lost thirty four pounds.
A total of twenty one and a half inches lost.**

**I actually wore a size four for several months but maintained a
size six.**

About the Author

SHAKISHA SHAMAIN EDNESS, a writer, mentor, motivational speaker, and evangelist for Christ. Speaking Truth, Changing Perception, and Gaining Lives to Christ by sharing her testimonies and word of God. She is from Newark, New Jersey and partially raised in Atlanta, Georgia. She found her passion through her pain, and then her pain directed her to her God's given purpose. She is truly an inspiration to others and she gives all the recognitions to Jesus!

Shakisha Edness is the CEO/Founder of TRA-C Inc., which is named after her beloved mother Tracie. TRA-C Inc. was founded in 2006. A nonprofit organization that is designed to educate and empower men, women, and children that are affected directly and indirectly by HIV/AIDS and drug/alcohol abuse. She has mentored men in Atlanta group homes sharing her testimonies and have mentored the youth of Paulding County Public School System.

She is also the CEO/Founder of Women Overcoming Weight-loss, which has touched the lives of many women, since it was founded in 2009. She ministers to women on a daily basis through a conference call prayer line, where she has seen blessings and miracles take place in many lives.

Shakisha became an Adolescent Peer Counselor under Sandra Mc Donald, the Founder of Outreach, Inc. Working side by side with her mother at age fifteen, sharing her story of an addict's child. Shakisha since then has pursued her career in motivational speaking, evangelizing, and writing to minister to those she may never get a chance to meet.

Shakisha is an extension of God's love without limits.

Author Contact Information

To purchase books, for more information, or to schedule
Shakisha Edness to speak, please contact:

Shakisha Edness

www.shakishaedness.com

Here's another nugget for the road. Remember we are all gardeners. So always be ready to uproot and replant. Pull the weeds out before they destroy your garden. A gardener does it all, plants the seed and waters the garden, but God provides the increase.

Do me a favor, join me in this movement. Help me plant a seed and/or water one that has been planted, by purchasing an extra copy of this book and sowing it into another person life. It can be a family member, friend, associate, enemy, and/or a complete stranger.

God bless your seeds.

www.ingramcontent.com/pod-product-compliance
Lightning Source LLC
LaVergne TN
LVHW051201080426
835508LV00021B/2741